SILENT WORKPLACE

Shops, stores, businesses, and factories where Hoosiers once earned a living

General Store (Was in the Lewis family from 1876 until it closed in 1992.), Lewisville—Morgan Co. (708.03)

Photography by John Bower

STUDIO INDIANA®

Text by John and Lynn Bower
Foreword by Gayle and Bill Cook

Published by:
Studio Indiana®
430 N. Sewell Road   Bloomington, IN 47408
(812) 332-5073   www.studioindiana.com

©2008, Printed in China

Publisher's Cataloging-in-Publication Data
Bower, John.
Silent Workplace: Shops, stores, businesses, and factories where Hoosiers once earned a living /
photography by John Bower;
text by John Bower and Lynn Bower;
foreword by Gayle Cook and Bill Cook.

p.   cm.
ISBN: 978-0-9745186-4-0
1. Commercial buildings—Indiana—Pictorial works.
2. Indiana—Pictorial works.
3. Architecture—Indiana.
4. Photography, Artistic.
I. Bower, John, 1949–.   II. Title.
TR659.6.B69   2008
779.944772—dc22
Library of Congress Control Number: 2007909737

FOREWORD

The "silent" workplaces that we've restored, reused, or torn down, have really been rather noisy places. In its own way, each has spoken loudly and clearly to us—just as the abandoned structures of John Bower's photographs do to those who care to listen. Every forlorn building tells something about the people and activities once sheltered there. In the buildings we've been involved with, we've found written messages, machines, tools, products, pigeons, rats, and mice, but more surprisingly, a sentimental legacy that is often overwhelming.

We expected an emotional local celebration when we rehabbed and reopened a tiny general store. It had been the only gathering place in a thirty-mile area. Laconia—Indiana's smallest town, according to the 2000 census—truly lost its soul when the business closed. Painfully missed—along with the convenient grocery staples—were the liars' bench, hot coffee, euchre games, lodge meetings, and the clerking job opportunities. That store restoration was one of our most diminutive, but most rewarding, projects because of the reviving effect it had on everyday lives.

We hadn't forecast the happy tears and smiles at the gala opening of our new facility in a long-empty Bloomington manufacturing plant. The former employees, of a factory that had been one of RCA's largest, reminisced about what once was, and prowled their cavernous old haunts for hours. To most of us, it was just another mammoth building, but to them it continues to hold a very significant place in their hearts and memories.

Even though it had not functioned as a hotel for seventy-five years, our restoration of the West Baden Springs Hotel, a National Historic Landmark, elicited an outpouring of affectionate guest and employee recollections. Nearly every family in West Baden Springs, and nearby French Lick, is connected in some way to that venerable building. Until the renovation, locals had resigned themselves to having their memories and precious old photographs outlive the ruins.

Be assured, each of John Bower's images shows just such a place, large or small, that has been an important part of the personal history of someone—boss, hourly worker, or customer.

Photographs—both vintage and contemporary—are most valuable to us during a renovation project because they capture every minuscule detail that will be important when the space is returned to its historic appearance. In this collection of photographs of silent workplaces, can be found—in the ambiance and details of windows, moldings, bricks and mortar, even nails—clues that communicate our valuable Indiana history. These buildings talk to us, without words, about our heritage, as well as the personalities of neighbors, parents, and grandparents who labored in them—for us.

Gayle and Bill Cook
Bloomington, Indiana
November 2007

4

Store, Salem—Adams Co. (754.09)

INTRODUCTION

I was about 4 years old when I was first exposed to the world of work. By myself, I was allowed to walk the four blocks from home to Dad's typewriter shop to watch him repair the machines. He made his living in a small, one-story, two-room building, located a half-block off 5th Street (the main drag) in the small northwestern Indiana town of Fowler.

Inside the Gregory R. Bower Co., there were new and refurbished Coronas, Underwoods, and Remingtons arranged in the front room on desks and tables so they could be admired by passersby through the large plate-glass window. In the back room, a heavy-duty steel workbench (which I now have in my garage) dominated one corner. There was also a tall cabinet (designed to hold printing type) filled with drawers of tiny spare parts, several storage shelves, an air compressor, a tub of cleaning solvent, a mimeograph machine, and a contraption that automatically folded paper.

To me, typewriters were magical, mechanical marvels. But when Dad was repairing one, he liked to work alone, and quietly—so my questions were considered distractions. Rather than explain what he was doing in terms I could grasp, he'd sit me down in front of an ancient, black, upright typewriter, along with a few sheets of paper, in the hope that I would entertain myself.

At first, I eagerly pecked away, learning how to rotate the rubber roller, figuring out how to make capital letters, even mastering an intriguing little lever that engaged the red half of the inked, two-tone ribbon. I especially liked the ding of the nickel-plated bell when the carriage reached the end of a line.

This was all great fun but, eventually, because I could only spell a few simple words, boredom would creep in. My fidgeting, and renewed questioning, would prompt Dad to suggest I go visit Conrad's Bakery—an excursion I couldn't resist. For me, the aromas of the warm bakery were always more inviting than the harsh cleaning-solvent odors wafting through Dad's place.

Conrad was Dad's favorite older brother, and his bakery was only a half-block away, just down on the corner. He was a bachelor, and we truly enjoyed each other's company. To my delight, he never minded answering my endless queries. As a result, I learned about making bread dough and pastries, how to open the oven doors and adjust the temperature, and how to clean up properly.

While he made all manner of baked goods, Uncle Conrad liked creating beautiful cakes the best. He was, in fact, a cake-decorating master—able to spread butter-cream frosting with a flourish. Fascinated, I'd watch him fill cone-shaped paper tubes with a spectrum of icings, then carefully squirt out pink rose petals, yellow squiggles, or the deep red, smooth, even lettering of a person's name. When he was done, he'd let me give it a try on a piece of cardboard, but all I ever made was a mess—but it was a mess I enjoyed eating afterwards. Years later, in my 50s, when I was putting this book together, I realized how my photography was a unique combination of what I witnessed as a young boy—the mechanical expertise of my Dad repairing typewriters and the creativity of Uncle Conrad in his bakery.

Back then (the early 1950s), there were no chain stores in Fowler (except the IGA), and many of the local citizens owned their own businesses. There was Cy the druggist, Fuzzy the lawyer, Joe the barber, and Johnny the junk man. But there were also people who worked for someone else—the gray-haired lady who clerked at the dime store, the friendly man who sold tickets at the theater, Walt and Tom the town's two cops, and Grandpa Mendy, who delivered mail on a circuitous rural route that wound through the Indiana countryside, and even dipped into Illinois.

It was an era when each town was unique, and every business had its own special character. Fowler, like many small towns, was fairly self-sufficient. You could do your banking, buy a suit, fresh produce, an oak dresser, or a new automobile. There was a theater, a hotel, and a small medical clinic. Because it wasn't a big place, many people walked the few blocks from their homes to work. A few citizens actually lived right where they made a living. Up until a few years before I was born, Mom's parents operated Dowell's Cafe, residing in the walk-up apartment directly above it.

In the midst of my childhood, we moved to Lafayette, a medium-sized Hoosier town. Mom and Dad believed it had more to offer than Fowler and, in many ways, it did. There were 5 theaters from which to choose and 2 drive-ins, more restaurants, a larger city park, and many streets and neighborhoods to explore. There were factories that produced wire (Peerless), gears (Fairfield), aluminum extrusions (Alcoa), jigsaw puzzles (Warren Paper) and prefab houses (National Homes).

6

At that time, Lafayette's downtown was vital and dynamic—filled with all manner of businesses housed in 2-, 3-, and 4-story brick and stone buildings. A few were chains such as Kresge's and Montgomery Ward. There was Loeb's Department Store (with the only escalator in town), Reifer's Furniture (with its neon rocking-chair sign that actually rocked), and McHaley Army Surplus. There were over a dozen clothing stores (including Three Sisters for women and the Baltimore for men), as well as jewelers, taverns, drug stores, banks, hotels—and five cigar stores. Many of these enterprises were owned by local folk. But even then, the times, they were a-changing.

When we moved to Lafayette, Dad set up his typewriter business, not downtown, but in Lafayette's first shopping center, Mar-Jean Village, a basic strip named for the developer's two daughters, Marge and Jean. Within just a few years, he moved again—to the more expansive, and beautifully landscaped, Market Square, when it opened in 1958. With Mom's input, lines of gifts, greeting cards, and party supplies were added, along with a classier name—Bower's of Market Square.

Today, both Fowler and Lafayette are quite different places than they were in my boyhood. As with many smaller communities, most of Fowler's businesses are now just memories. The town's population has remained fairly stable, but it's been quite a while since the downtown was a thriving center of commerce. There are several vacant lots where stores once stood, Dad's old typewriter shop among them. It was razed decades ago.

Unlike Fowler, Lafayette—like many mid-sized towns—has grown and sprawled out into the surrounding countryside. But, despite it's vibrancy, many of the new businesses are chains and franchises. Loeb's Department Store is gone, and Reifer's went out of business long ago—its rocking-chair sign removed. Three of the theaters from my childhood no longer exist, and the other two quit showing movies. The downtown has no drugstores, shoe stores, or hardware stores. They've been replaced with offices, antique and gift emporiums, and a few up-scale eateries and coffee shops. And Bower's of Market Square no longer exists.

In Lafayette, as in other cities and towns, most of the retail, factory, and office buildings erected in recent decades are the same clones you see everywhere—sterile, nondescript concrete-block rectangles, with a little low-cost glitz and glamour added. The trademarked color schemes and graphic logos are the marks of faceless global corporations. I doubt anyone will admire these cookie-cutter buildings in the future, and feel compelled to say, "Save these for posterity!"

While many of today's businesses offer convenience and celebrity endorsements, they lack the unique character of those places I knew as a kid. I miss the squeaky wooden floors of the dime store and the elevator operator in the Lafayette Life Building who would ask what floor I wanted. I miss the old theatres—The Luna, The Main, and The State—that have been replaced by multiplexes. And, I miss seeing my neighbors' names on business signs, and the personal attention they so readily gave all their customers.

So, for this book, I decided to focus my camera on those empty, sometimes eccentric, old buildings where Hoosiers used to earn their livings—places that had been proud, filled with energy, bristling with hustle and bustle, but now sit idle and forlorn. Some of these businesses have been closed for only a short time, others for as many as 50 years—or more. Each is still, quiet—yet they all have stories to tell.

On the following pages, are portraits of a variety of former workplaces—factories, mills, shops, offices, and stores. They are where we, our parents, and our grandparents once toiled, sometimes happily, sometimes enduringly—then walked

away from, never to return. Some of these now desolate buildings will, in time, be fixed up or restored and have a new life, a new purpose. Others will eventually be torn down and cease to be. My photographs are images of temporary, ephemeral places—caught on film between what they were and what they will eventually become.

Most of these tired and worn edifices were erected years ago—in some cases back in the 19th century, well before my time. Back then, commercial buildings were designed to last for 100 years or more—not just the 20 or 30 years of today's modern boxes. Many are still stately and solid, built of Indiana limestone or of bricks fired in nearby kilns, with lumber sawn in local mills, by workmen from the surrounding area. Exuberant gingerbread exteriors displaying a family name, and interiors with elaborate tin ceilings, flamboyantly reflect the personalities and status of sole proprietors.

Because these buildings are so infused with pride, they radiate an emotional, as well as a visual, attraction to me. They have served us well over the decades, and they need to be paid attention to, respected, honored, and treasured. I feel this very strongly—they are an endangered, yet integral, part of our history, of Indiana's cultural and economic heritage.

For me, the past really comes alive when I set up my tripod in front of a boarded-up, small-town store. I think about the people who interacted there in its heyday. I wonder about the original owner who, like Dad or Uncle Conrad, grew up a few miles away, went to the local high school, started the business on a shoestring, and slowly built up a clientele. He (occasionally, she) was responsible for unlocking the door in the morning, working long hours, waiting on customers, taking inventory, kibitzing with traveling salesmen, placing special orders, handling the inevitable complaints, sweeping the floors, and keeping the books. Ultimately, the success or failure rested on their shoulders—alone.

When I carry my camera through a defunct factory—such as a mill or workshop where hard, manual labor was the norm—I can almost hear the loud repetitive noises, feel the aching muscles, sense the sweat on my brow. I can imagine the cursing when a finger was smashed; laughter from a practical joke played on the new guy; sighs of satisfied relief at the end of a long, difficult job well done; and stoic condolences after a fellow worker was killed on the job. Whether a well-paying factory, or one that doled out starvation wages, it was where a person (usually a man) earned enough (perhaps barely enough) to pay for food, clothing, and shelter for himself and his family—if he had one. It was where he spent much of his adult life. It was central to his identity, of how he thought of himself and how others thought of him.

Despite the poignancy and unnatural silence that shrouds these stores, shops, and factories, I'm very aware of an earthy liveliness, vigor, and sense of fulfillment that once electrified the air. These were places of human activity—of calloused hands and calculating minds. These were times before computers or bar codes, when receipts were written with a fountain pen—or typed on a typewriter. Communication was exchanged with letters and stamps, instead of terse, misspelled emails. Because there were few packaged foods, restaurant workers peeled potatoes and shucked corn by hand for noontime diners. Kids picked out penny candy at the corner drug store by pointing a finger and saying, "Two of those, one of those, three of those," as an aproned clerk sacked each sugary confection—piece, by piece, by piece. That genuine, direct, visceral, humanness is often missing from many of today's workplaces.

Of course, it was not a perfect world. In the "olden days," machinery could be extremely dangerous, with safety requirements ranging from minimal to non-existent. Yet, if you broke your arm, you knew the "Doc" who wrapped it up in a wet-plaster-and-cotton-gauze cast. He answered his own telephone, and he made house calls. When I was a child living in Fowler, if the fire department's siren went off, I could dial "oper" on our black Bakelite phone, and the operator would tell me whose house was ablaze.

Without a doubt, there are very real advantages of today's workplaces—minimum wage, higher productivity, nondiscrimination laws, air conditioning, OSHA, the 40-hour work week, and Social Security benefits. However, there are losses that should not be underestimated. Today, few franchises have strong ties to the communities they reside in. And, as mom-and-pop businesses have declined, so has the belief that "the customer is always right."

I know we can't go backwards, nor should we. However, the past must not be dismissed as mere nostalgia. If we look closely, the rusted metal and peeling paint of old storefronts and empty factories can reveal much about those who came before us—how they lived, how they worked, and what was important to them. With this knowledge, we can better understand ourselves. For only by respecting and appreciating their choices and life circumstances can we objectively judge our own.

I'm pleased to honor on these pages, all the empty, dusty, commercial buildings that are scattered across Indiana, and the businesses they once housed—barber shops, general stores, flour mills, furniture factories, leather tanneries, gas stations, creameries, and theaters—with a special homage to a small, one-story, two-room typewriter repair shop, and a nearby bakery, where a four-year old boy watched and learned how grown men earned a living.

John Bower

9

MidStates Wire Co. (Parts of this building date from the early 1900s. It was closed and abandoned in the late 1990s, and suffered two fires in 2003.), Crawfordsville—Montgomery Co. (743.05)

10

Don Meyers Automotive, Liberty Mills—Wabash Co. (765.06)

11

Barber Shop, Patricksburg—Owen Co. (706.01)

12

Store, Dunreith—Henry Co. (769.13)

Store, Lynnville—Warrick Co. (785.03)

Store, Carlos—Randolph Co. (770.03)

Fortwendel General Store (Limestone sidewalk.),
Troy—Perry Co. (748.03)

Store, Charlottesville—Hancock Co. (780.15)

13

Murl May Garage (Built around 1912, closed in 1962.), Salamonia—Jay Co. (756.07)

14

Hays Grocery (and gas), Sanders—Monroe Co. (735.02)

FROM THE CANAL ERA

When I visited the Connersville Furniture Co., I was impressed. It was an imposing six-story building—50 feet by 150 feet. First opened for business in 1882, a five-story factory was soon added, as well as a pair of five-story additions. The company produced black-walnut bedroom furniture. Later, other lines were added, with some constructed of imported woods. Today, only the original red-brick structure remains.

The nearby Whitewater Canal was a cheap and handy energy source for the plant. Water diverted from a nearby basin turned a large paddle wheel to power the factory. After passing over the wheel, most of the current flowed through four race channels underneath the building, then returned to the canal. But some of the water was retained and was used for steam generation.

Connersville Furniture Co., Connersville—Fayette Co. (733.12)

In the 1950s, the Roots Division of Dresser Industries, Inc. purchased the site to produce and repair wooden patterns for its foundry. The building is now owned, and being restored, by the Community Education Coalition, Inc. for its own offices, and rental space for other organizations.

When I photographed the structure, most of the exterior restoration had been completed—the brickwork was repaired, a new roof was in place, and 330 small-paned windows had been fixed or replaced. Inside, the interior had been cleaned out, but not yet refurbished.

I admired the massive wooden beams and joists. The first floor columns (right) were especially sturdy so they could support all the loads on the upper floors. As I ascended the well-worn stairs, and finally reached the sixth story, I was immediately drawn to a window—and a spectacular view below.

16

Connersville Furniture Co. (Stairs.) Connersville—Fayette Co. (733.07)

Connersville Furniture Co. (Main floor.), Connersville—Fayette Co. (733.06)

17

Stores, Macy—Miami Co. (784.11)

19

Huff Furnace & Pump Co., Sullivan—Sullivan Co. (786.15)

Excavator bucket and arm—rural Clay Co. (088.02)

21

Excavator, Padanaram Commune—Martin Co. (104.12)

Stores, Leavenworth—Crawford Co. (724.13)

23

Store—rural Brown Co. (700.12)

A Landmark Closes

In mid-2007, the Citizens Gas and Coke Utility announced it would close its coke manufacturing plant in Indianapolis. The facility—a landmark on Prospect St.—was originally built in 1908 to produce both coke and gas from coal.

Coke—a manufactured product—is burned in steel mills, blast furnaces, and foundries. Considered a better fuel than coal, it releases fewer sulphurous compounds and creates less smoke. Coke is derived from coal that is baked at high temperatures. During this process, water, coal-gas, and coal-tar are driven off as by-products. The coal-tar can be processed further into a variety of marketable materials. The other principle by-product, coal-gas (also called coke-oven gas, or manufactured gas), can be used to heat homes and businesses.

Until the 1950s, most of Indianapolis was heated with coal-gas that was produced at this location. Then, when natural gas arrived in the area from other parts of the country through interstate pipelines, the coal-gas operation began to be phased out. By 1998, natural gas had completely replaced coal-gas for heating homes and businesses. The coke itself remained a viable product—until foreign competition led to a declining market share

When I photographed the plant, it was in the process of being decommissioned. Then, any environmental problems that remained would be cleaned up. Finally, because Citizens couldn't find a buyer for the operation, it would be razed. The closing is bittersweet for the 300 employees who will need to find new jobs. But others in

Citizens Gas & Coke Plant, Indianapolis—
Marion Co. (798.09)

Citizens Gas & Coke Plant, Indianapolis—
Marion Co. (797.14)

the neighborhood are looking forward to a time when the odors emanating from the manufacture of coke, coal-gas, and all the other products, will be gone. For them, it will, literally, be a breath of fresh air.

Citizens Gas & Coke Plant, Indianapolis—
Marion Co. (798.13)

Citizens Gas & Coke Plant, Indianapolis—
Marion Co. (798.06)

Citizens Gas & Coke Plant (gas storage), Indianapolis—
Marion Co. (565.01)

27

28

Singer Manufacturing Co. (Singer's first sewing–machine factory in South Bend was built in 1868. This building was erected around 1901 and was closed in 1954.), South Bend—St. Joseph Co. (772.12)

29

Singer Manufacturing Co. (This building was part of a 76 acre site dedicated to building wooden sewing-machines cases.), South Bend—St. Joseph Co. (772.09)

30

Thomas Hardware Store (Was the location of the local Post Office, and once sold Shell gasoline. Closed in 1992.), Grass Creek—Fulton Co. (795.08)

Thomas Hardware Store (In 1902, this was the 2nd John Deere dealership in Indiana.),
Grass Creek—Fulton Co. (795.10)

Beyers Unique Shop (Auto/Boat Upholstery Shop.), Clear Creek—Monroe Co. (765.15)

Farmer's Dairy, Carlos—Randolph Co. (770.05)

Cora's Coiffures, Marengo—Crawford Co. (747.10)

THE MAKING OF A MUSEUM

When Neil Strock looked at a closed-up business called The Butler Company (in Butler, Indiana), he saw far more than a defunct factory. He saw tremendous potential. So, he did something most of us would never consider. In 1999, he bought the place—lock, stock, and barrel—so it could be converted into a museum.

It didn't take long for Neil to round up a dedicated Board of Directors, who obtained non-profit status for The National Heartland Agricultural and Industrial Power Museum. Then the real work began—cleaning, repairing, maintaining, and collecting. While the Museum isn't yet open to the public, the project is well under way.

The Butler Co., Butler—DeKalb Co. (753.07)

The Butler Company (founded as the Butler Manufacturing Company in 1888) was best known for producing windmills. In 1997, it officially closed down. During the intervening decades, it made a wide variety of products, including high-quality bicycles (with either wood or steel handlebars, but no coaster brake), and a few early Star automobiles. In 1930, it cvcn produced an experimental airplane called the Yellow Jacket. The Museum has been collecting as many examples of Butler-built products as it can lay its hands on.

There are several versions of Butler windmills (including a set of blades 8-feet in diameter), Butler pumps for both windmills and cisterns, and two Butler buggies, circa 1910. While most of the original manufacturing equipment has disappeared, I was pleased to see a hulking old cupola—a type of blast furnace used for casting metal—that was still intact.

When I first looked at the heavily worn treads of the stairway leading up to the third floor, I was imagining how many feet had traveled up and down them. Then Neil pointed out something I hadn't spotted. Every tread was hinged, and there was a storage compartment under each step.

The Museum is also interested in displaying agricultural and industrial products manufactured elsewhere, but during the same era The Butler Company was thriving. I was impressed with the mechanical complexity of the threshing machine—a horse-drawn Birdsell model. There's also a nice collection of small gasoline engines.

The Museum has accomplished a great deal in a short period of time—but there's still work to do. Portions of the exterior brickwork require a mason's attention, some windows need replacing, and there's more collecting to do. But, it's definitely on its way—and I'm pleased to have had a sneak preview.

The Butler Co. (Stairs.), Butler—DeKalb Co. (779.06)

The Butler Co. (Portable Fairbanks scales.), Butler—DeKalb Co. (779.07)

The Butler Co. (Cupola, for melting metal.), Butler—DeKalb Co. (778.15)

The Butler Co. (Oven, for baking the sand cores used in casting metal.), Butler—DeKalb Co. (778.12)

35

Barber Shop, Coal City—Owen Co. (706.04)

37

Barber Shop, Kurtz—Jackson Co. (696.08)

Warren Paper Products (Built around 1890. Originally the Indiana Wagon Co., which produced 30 wagons a day. Warren Paper manufactured jigsaw puzzles), Lafayette—Tippecanoe Co. (720.15)

39

Golden Castings (Founded as Columbus Foundry Co. in 1915. This oven, for baking the sand cores used in casting metal, to harden and strengthen them, was in a building constructed in 1924, and razed in 2007.), Columbus—Bartholomew Co. (544.03)

40

Citizens State Bank, Lagro—Wabash Co. (793.07)

41

Farmers State Bank, Wolcottville—LaGrange Co. (777.04)

Forsaken Domes

The Historic Landmarks Foundation of Indiana placed the Medora Brick Plant on its list of 10 Most Endangered Landmarks in 2004. Opened in 1906, the factory once produced 54,000 bricks a day, and employed 50 people. Now, it's in decay.

John and I found the place magical. Stretching across a flat, overgrown several acres, there were smokestacks and a dozen round, yurt-shaped structures. Known as "beehive" kilns, they were heated by coal, until 1992, when EPA regulations led to the operation being closed.

We found the kilns fascinating. Each was banded with heavy iron strapping to prevent expansion when it was heated. Two arched doors, used for loading bricks, provided access to the interior. When we entered one kiln, and saw the domed brick ceiling overhead, it felt as if we were in some ancient place of worship.

Later, we explored other parts of the factory—a brick drying building, sheds, an office, and a maintenance facility. At one time, for Halloween, the locals created "haunted" scenes inside the empty structures. We found a few decorations still lying about.

Some day, these ruins at Medora will be completely gone. Yet, the bricks manufactured here will endure—in the walls of buildings, and under layers of asphalt in roads, all across the Midwest.

Medora Brick Plant, Medora—Jackson Co. (074.15)

Medora Brick Plant (Access door.), Medora—Jackson Co. (425.11)

43

Grocery Store, Farmersburg—Sullivan Co. (706.09)

Stores, Howe—LaGrange Co. (753.14)

46

One-Room Diner (An outhouse sits by the back fence.), West Melcher—Parke Co. (704.06)

47

"The Keg" Root-Beer Stand (Closed 1962.)—rural Orange Co. (699.14)

E. C. Schleyer Pump Company (Previously part of American Steel and Wire.), Anderson—Madison Co. (718.12)

Royer Wheelworks (Later Alton Box Company.), Aurora—Dearborn Co. (738.15)

Brookville Manufacturing Co. (A candy & canning factory. Later Wilson Feed Store.), Brookville—Franklin Co. (739.05)

Muessel Brewing Co. (Founded in 1852, acquired by Drewry's in 1936.), South Bend—St. Joseph Co. (773.13)

Indiana Statuary Co., Indianapolis—Marion Co. (476.10)

50

Poneto Hardware Co., Poneto—Wells Co. (768.07)

Store, Larwill—Whitley Co. (765.03)

GOOD FOR WHAT AILED YOU

Christmas Day 1890 was a particularly special one for the small community of Kramer. On that day, The Hotel Mudlavia, an opulent health spa, opened for business. Situated near a natural spring, the Warren County showplace offered mineral-laden drinking water and soothing mud baths.

"Mudlavia Moor Mud" was famous. It was said to be good for rheumatism, arthritis, as well as a host of other chronic conditions. The mud was excavated from an adjacent hillside, mixed with water, and heated. After reaching the proper consistency and temperature, it was ready to slather on eager guests.

Mudlavia (Boiler.), Kramer—
Warren Co. (745.15)

Then, on a cold February day in 1920, the spa was consumed by fire. But several years later, in 1934, a new, smaller Mudlavia rose, Phoenix-like, from the ashes. For a while, the resort thrived—then it went through a period of closings and reopenings, and eventually became a restaurant. In 1974, fire struck once more, and it's been a ruin ever since.

52

Over the years, many famous people signed Mudlavia's guest register, including such notables as John L. Sullivan, James Whitcomb Riley, and Paul Dresser. One patron, not so well known, was my grandmother. I have a postcard, with a black-and-white image of Mudlavia on the front, that Grandma mailed from there, to my other grandmother, in 1949.

The message reads: "This is the life of Riley. If I could just quit hurting at all it would be swell. I am getting better and hope to be out the end of the week. Will stay till I feel OK. Hope you are better. Maybe this would be good for you. See you soon."

I didn't come across the old postcard until long after Grandma died—so I couldn't ask her about the visit. But, her words imply that she received relief from some ailment. I hope so.

Lynn and I first wandered through Mudlavia's once-manicured grounds in the late 1970s. Even in its run down state, we could tell it had been a remarkable place. When we returned recently, the site was much more overgrown and the building was far more deteriorated. The interior walls were covered in graffiti, and everything of value had been taken. I did find some dilapidated, rusting equipment in the old boiler room that was probably used for heating water—and the famous mud.

Surprisingly, Mudlavia is still a popular place to visit. During the hour Lynn and I were taking pictures, four other cars arrived loaded with adults and children. One couple warned us that the place was haunted. Perhaps it is, but no mud-covered apparitions appeared on my film.

Mudlavia (Second floor.), Kramer—Warren Co. (745.12)

Mudlavia (Main floor.), Kramer—Warren Co. (745.06)

53

Third Strike Saloon, Montezuma—Parke Co. (703.15)

55

Red & White Quality Foods, Montezuma—Parke Co. (704.04)

Scott Manufacturing Co. (This metal fabrication plant was closed in 1997.), Scottsburg—Scott Co. (698.04)

56

57

Mt. Vernon [hominy] Milling Co. (Detroit Rotostoker boiler.), Mt. Vernon—Posey Co. (679.07)

58

Tell City Auto & Machine Works, Tell City—Perry Co. (747.13)

"We sell cloth shades, Joanna Western Mills," Greensburg—Decatur Co. (734.13)

59

FOUR GENERATIONS

It was a moment of mixed emotions for Phil Robertson, as he unlocked the door to his old mill. This had been a family business—owned and operated by Robertsons for four generations. But recently, the property had been auctioned off. The final closing would take place in a few days. Now, as Phil showed John and me around, it was obvious how proud he was of this place.

"My great grandfather started this mill back in 1880, along with four other fellows," Phil explained. It was called the Ewing Mill Co., but that eventually changed to The Robertson Corporation. It's located along a Jackson Co. rail line in what was once the town of Ewing. In 1967, after its post office closed, Ewing became part of Brownstown.

The Robertson Corp., Brownstown—Jackson Co. (758.07)

After entering, I saw that the interior of the mill was vast, with high ceilings held up by solid wood beams and towering columns. In the center of the room, stood a row of four roller mills, each with snaking aluminum tubes leading elsewhere. I was especially impressed with their wood cases, which had viewing windows. Phil pointed to the end one, saying it was just like the one his family had donated to the Smithsonian Institution.

For years, the entire Ewing operation had been powered by steam. Downstairs Phil showed us the boiler in a back room. It was a massive, cast-iron beast, originally fired by wood—later by coal and corn cobs. The steam engine itself was long gone, having been scrapped during WW II. Phil picked up an old pressure gauge lying nearby. Slowly, he looked it over. It held many memories. Almost reverently, he placed it back down.

I mentioned how much I admired the heavy wood columns—assuming they were original. "No," Phil said, "Those were put up in '42 after a fire gutted part of the mill." It's believed a spark from a passing locomotive caused the conflagration.

Phil next revealed a bit about himself. He went to Kansas State University, graduating from the

The Robertson Corp. (Milling room.), Brownstown—Jackson Co. (763.10)

The Robertson Corp. (Boiler.), Brownstown—
Jackson Co. (764.07)

The Robertson Corp. (Basement.), Brownstown—
Jackson Co. (764.06)

country's only degree program in milling, then served in the Air Force. When he returned to Ewing, he started reworking the mill's equipment. When he was done, the mill's efficiency was increased threefold.

Phil informed us that, over the years, the mill had ground a variety of grains—producing animal feed, dog food, and enriched flour. However, in recent years, their main product had been Glu-X—a wheat-based additive used as an extending agent for plywood adhesives.

Phil sighed, sharing with us how it had been a tough decision to sell this place. But, the fifth generation of Robertsons had successful careers in other fields. At one time, his family had owned mills in several southern Indiana communities, including Bedford, Jeffersonville, and Seymour. This one in Ewing was their first, and their last. An era was ending.

The Robertson Corp. (Power belts.), Brownstown—
Jackson Co. (764.08)

61

62

Rogers Concrete Block Plant, Bloomington—Monroe Co. (735.14)

Ice House, Cloverdale—Putnam Co. (491.08)

Kahler Furniture Factory (Later National Homes Corp.), New Albany—Floyd Co. (728.06)

Kahler Furniture Factory (Later National Homes Corp.), New Albany—Floyd Co. (728.04)

65

Armours Creamery (Became Crystal Dairy in the 1960s.), Rochester—Fulton Co. (784.02)

66

General Store (Later an Antique Store.), Millhousen—Decatur Co. (732.05)

Maegerlein Flouring Mill, (Later Dubois Brothers Lumber.), Patricksburg—Owen Co. (736.04)

67

SAVING THE OPERA HOUSE

When Lynn Corson called to order a few of our Studio Indiana books, he mentioned an old building that we might like to photograph. It contained a third-floor opera house in the Carroll County community of Delphi. He said it was a space that had been unused for nearly 100 years. It sounded intriguing, so John and I made plans to visit.

When we parked our car in front of the three-story, Italianate edifice, Anita Werling, President of the Delphi Preservation Society, was already waiting for us. After introducing herself, she explained that the Society had owned two-thirds

Delphi Opera House (Steps at rear of tiers.),
Delphi—Carroll Co. (788.02)

of the large building in front of us for several years, and had recently been able to purchase the remaining third. She then described the exterior restoration work that was already underway. They were getting rid of all the inappropriate remodeling that had been added over the years, installing new wood dentil trim, and they had a crew busy scraping and painting the upper windows.

However, Anita added, there was much more to be done—and some of it was structural. Several sagging scissor roof trusses had to be lifted and reinforced, and the roof itself needed replacing. She went on to explain how the front façade would look like it did in the early 1900s. "We can't go back to how it appeared when it was built in the 1860s. Too much has happened to the building for that."

Anita then opened a nondescript door. In the dim light, we saw an intimidating flight of wide, very steep, wooden stairs, leading upwards. "Can you imagine ladies in high-button shoes and long dresses ascending these?" she mused. I couldn't—it was difficult enough for me in jeans and sneakers. Anita said that, years ago, this opera house was closed for good because, after a fire damaged a nearby opera house, the local Fire Marshall feared these stairs would make for a poor fire escape.

When we reached the second-floor landing, we stopped in front of a pair of tall, blackened-with-age, moss-green doors. Anita unlatched one, swung it open, and we climbed another set of stairs, more narrow than the others, in darker

68

Delphi Opera House (Balcony view.), Delphi—Carroll Co. (788.07)

light. At yet another landing, we turned, climbed a few more steps, and were, at last, inside the Opera House proper, looking toward the stage.

In a word, it was awesome—an open, lofty space, but one with a musty look, and a musty smell. Down front, the raised, curtainless stage had a crumbling Venetian mural as a permanent backdrop. Both the street- and alley-side walls had tall, narrow windows alternating with sections of discolored wallpaper depicting swimming swans. On the ceiling, amid layers of flaking paint and paper, were affixed three, large, plaster medallions painted red and green. From our position at the rear of the Opera House, the dark wooden floor descended in several shallow tiers. There were a few sections of folding wooden seats with arabesque, iron frames, which I learned were not original to the building

As we walked forward, then looked up behind us, we spotted the narrow balcony. It appeared that most of its cast-iron decoration was missing. "The previous owner removed it," Anita explained, "and, it was a good thing, too. That metal adornment was so heavy, the entire balcony could have collapsed if he hadn't."

Directly below the balcony, I spotted the remains of three pigeons laid out on a platter. Before I could ask, Anita anticipated my question. "Oh, those. They were found when we cleaned up the bird droppings. A member of our group likes to collect animal skeletons, so we saved them." Of course.

Our hostess next led us up onto the stage itself, and informed us, "You know, this building was called City Hall, but not because it held municipal offices. It never did. The name referred to this large hall, or opera house, with its expansive, flat seating area. It wasn't until 1882 that the tiers were added to the floor, and the stage was extended." Anita pointed to a tin-lined trough running all along the front edge of the stage, "We think that's where lime was burned to create a glowing bright light. You know—limelight," she said, with a twinkle in her eye.

Delphi Opera House (Stage.), Delphi—Carroll Co. (787.11)

Stepping back down, John set up his camera and start shooting, while Anita showed me the architectural plans the Society had had prepared. They were quite extensive: an addition would be built on the rear of the building for such modern amenities as a kitchen, elevators, rest rooms, and a grand lobby with a brand-new entrance.

The third-floor opera-house space would be completely renovated, with its original level floor restored. That way, a dinner theater and wedding receptions could be accommodated. There would also be new dressing rooms, along with exhibition and archival display areas on the second floor. This was indeed ambitious, yet it was also do-able—if they could raise enough money.

After the three of us descended back down to street level, Anita gave us a brief tour of some other historic downtown buildings. As we walked up to Delphi's former interurban station, she pointed downward, "That's Deer Creek, the one James Whitcomb Riley wrote about." Then, she beamed, "He was at our opera house on six occasions."

Delphi Opera House (Backstage door.), Delphi—Carroll Co. (787.12)

Delphi Opera House (Seating.), Delphi—Carroll Co. (787.14)

72

Buchannan General Store and gasoline station (Prior to 1931, this building housed a Post Office and a tavern. After the 1950s, it was briefly a restaurant), Hovey—Posey Co. (514.10)

Automobile Garage, Raymond—Franklin Co. (734.08)

74

Restaurant at the Maxville Pool, Maxville—Randolph Co. (770.07)

A&W Root-Beer Stand (Later a Barber Shop.), near North Vernon—Jennings Co. (802.03)

"The Hut" Drive-In Restaurant, Plainville—
Daviess Co. (786.03)

"The Hut" Drive-In Restaurant, Plainville—
Daviess Co. (786.04)

Fort Harrison Savings (Established April 18, 1896, razed in 2005.), Terre Haute—Vigo Co. (475.04)

Times Building (*Brazil Times* newspaper.), Brazil—Clay Co. (746.14)

Indiana Brass Company (Founded in 1911. Had been one of the community's oldest businesses.), Frankfort—Clinton Co. (710.15)

Moser Leather Co. (This tannery opened in 1864, and closed 2002. These six-foot diameter tanning drums, made of very hard Australian jarrah wood, were used for washing and processing leather.), New Albany—Floyd Co. (727-07)

AFTER THE FLOOD

Child Craft Industries, widely known for its children's furniture—cribs, dressers, and accessories—was once a major manufacturer in Salem. Then, in the summer of 2004, the town suffered a devastating flood when the Blue River overflowed its banks. Built in the flood plain, Child Craft's 750,000-square-foot building was, for a time, under five feet of water.

When I visited the factory, I could see large areas of buckled flooring where the flood had heaved the foundation. It looked like a roller coaster—or a Surrealist painting. All told, there was $12 million worth of damage.

Child Craft Industries, Salem—Washington Co. (751.05)

Child Craft Industries, Salem—Washington Co. (759.15)

Knowing the facility could not recover, the company salvaged what it could. Tons of machinery, that had served faithfully for decades, was sold as scrap. To survive, it purchased an existing woodworking operation, 23 miles away in New Salisbury, and Child Craft left Salem behind.

Founded in 1911, the plant had grown and prospered for years—in the 1990s it had as many as 650 employees. But, at the time of the flood, employment was down to 250. Today, most of the original structure is empty, with only a portion used for storage, and another area occupied by a recycling business. Many former employees have transferred to New Salisbury.

This was a place with a long history, where proud and skilled workers created quality products—a place where fathers and sons worked side by side. But it could not escape the ravages of Mother Nature.

Child Craft Industries, Salem—Washington Co. (749.14)

81

Child Craft Industries, Salem—Washington Co. (751.02)

82

Lambert's Garage (Parts room.), Morgantown—Johnson Co. (121.04)

SAFE LOAD
280# SQ. FT.

EXIT →

Carol Cook Dress Factory, Greensburg—Decatur Co. (731.08)

Store, Boswell—Benton Co. (731.02)

Decatur Castings (Had been in business for almost 90 years.), Decatur—Adams Co. (754.15)

Eagle Cotton Mills Co. (Built in 1884, to manufacture "sheetings, seamless bags, twines, carpet and other warps, hosiery yarn and batting, etc." Later housed Meese, Inc.), Madison—Jefferson Co. (736.13)

Natural Ovens Bakery (This self-supporting, monolithic dome is 220' in diameter and 23" thick at its base. It was erected in 2001. The Bakery closed in 2003.), Valparaiso—Porter Co. (693.04)

Ski-Hi Drive-In Theaters (Opened in 1952 with 2 screens, and could accommodate 500 cars. It was closed in 2005.), near Royerton—Delaware Co. (769.08)

RESEARCHING A PAST

There was nothing in this factory to indicate what it had been before being abandoned, so I asked at a neighboring business if anyone could remember. I was told "It *might* have been National Lead." But they weren't sure. So I contacted a reference librarian in Indianapolis, who looked up the address in an old City Directory, and she told me the building had been occupied by the American Bearing Corp. for several decades.

With a name like American Bearing, it sounded like a rather mundane operation. But an internet search revealed that it had done work for the government's Nuclear Weapons Program. Well, that perked my interest, so I delved further and learned that the property had been inspected and, according to guidelines published by the Nuclear Regulatory Commission, it posed no danger from radiation. Lynn and I had spent about an hour there on two different occasions, so that was certainly a relief.

A last bit of library research indicated that American Bearing had been owned by National Lead Corp. I could find no reference to either company after 1971, when they were apparently involved in a pollution-related lawsuit. I still don't know what they did there—and I'm not sure I want to.

American Bearing, Indianapolis—Marion Co. (056.12)

American Bearing, Indianapolis—Marion Co. (119.12)

American Bearing, Indianapolis—Marion Co. (119.08)

American Bearing, Indianapolis—Marion Co. (120.06)

89

90

Dutch Mill Service Station, Disko—Fulton Co. (782.04)

Buchanan Store, New Winchester—Hendricks Co. (705.01)

Store, Oakland City—Gibson Co. (790.12)

Store, Hope—Bartholomew Co. (747.05)

Store, South Whitley—Whitley Co. (775.12)

Store, Eminence—Morgan Co. (707.15)

Store, Mill Creek—LaPorte Co. (763.08)

93

94

Normandy Farms Dairy, Indianapolis—Marion Co. (719.12)

95

Normandy Farms Dairy, Indianapolis—Marion Co. (719.04)

C.E. Cummings General Store (Closed in 1970.), Norman Station—Jackson Co. (696.03)

General Store, Grange Corner—Parke Co. (729.15)

CHARLES HALL'S INVENTION

It was in 1896 that Charles Hall began his rock-melting experiments in Alexandria. Within a short period of time, he had invented a brand new product called rock wool—and erected a factory on the south side of town to manufacture it. Rock wool (also called mineral wool) is made by blowing steam through molten limestone to produce fine strands of insulation. It soon became widely used for both insulation and soundproofing.

In 1897 Hall formed his first business—Crystal Chemical Co. By 1906, he had built a new factory and changed the name to Banner Rock Products. This structure was made almost entirely of con-

Banner Rock Products (Plant #1.),
Alexandria—Madison Co. (717.14)

crete—except for the roof. It was partially ripped off by a tornado in 1922. This was Plant #1. Because the demand for rock-wool insulation continued to grow, it was followed by a larger, more modern Plant #2, on the north side of town.

In January 1929 (only months before the Great Depression), Hall sold his business to Johns-Manville Corp.—then the largest producer of insulation in the world. Soon it built a new, larger facility and, eventually, the old Banner Rock buildings were retired. Today, Manville—widely known as a manufacturer of fiberglass insulation—no longer has any operations in Alexandria.

As I took pictures, I saw only a few pieces of equipment scattered about—a beat-up file cabinet, part of an old blower, piles of pallets, a mangled bicycle. In Plant #2, I found a single locker sitting, forlornly, inside one of the cavernous buildings. It made the emptiness seem more poignant.

98

Banner Rock Products (Plant #2.),
Alexandria—Madison Co. (797.04)

99

Banner Rock Products (Plant #1.), Alexandria—Madison Co. (718.01)

Movie Projector (Strand Theater, opened in 1916, closed in 2004. Currently undergoing restoration.), Shelbyville—Shelby Co. (715.02)

103

Tivoli Theater (Opened on New Year's Eve in 1928, closed in 1998.), Spencer—Owen Co. (723.07)

Midstates Wire (Parts of this building date from the early 1900s. It was closed and abandoned in the late 1990s, and suffered two fires in 2003.), Crawfordsville—Montgomery Co. (743.01)

Jasper Cabinet Co. (Closed in 2002, after 98 years in business.), Jasper—Dubois Co. (748.05)

Williams House Hotel (Built in the early 1900s. To be razed after asbestos removal has been completed.) Worthington—Greene Co. (724.01)

106

Store, Stones Crossing—Johnson Co. (780.08)

Store, Leavenworth—Crawford Co. (724.10)

IDLE STONE MILLS

The first commercial limestone quarry was opened in Monroe County in 1827. Since then, quarries have opened, and closed, all over Lawrence and Monroe Counties—as well as the mills, where the stone was shaped. Today, there are a number of limestone mills that remain profitable businesses. However, others didn't make it. Some have left no trace, while a few buildings have been converted to other uses.

Over the last several years, I've photographed three abandoned limestone mills—all in Monroe County—that still had equipment sitting in them. One had shut down in the 1970s, the other two more recently. The images on these four pages were taken at all three locations.

When I photographed these old limestone mills, I was struck by their size—they were often as large as football fields. Inside the soaring spaces, there were massive saws and planers set up to cut, and precisely shape, rough-cut blocks into finished products for architects and builders. For years, this equipment operated on steam power but, eventually, the steam engines were replaced with powerful electric motors. And skilled carvers and artisans who relied exclusively on chisels and mallets began to use pneumatic equipment.

Limestone Mill (Electrical panel.), Bloomington—Monroe Co. (128.10)

108

Limestone Mill (Crane operator cabin.),
Bloomington—Monroe Co. (051.05)

Limestone Mill (Forge.), Bloomington—Monroe Co.
(043.13)

Limestone Mill (Hook.)—Monroe Co.(101.02)

Limestone Mill, Bloomington—Monroe Co. (424.10)

109

With its even texture, uniform color, and overall quality, Indiana limestone has been used to build many important commercial and public buildings. These include the Empire State Building and the Pentagon, as well as state capitols, courthouses, university classrooms, churches, schools, and other structures all across the country.

As I took my photographs, I had the impression that the equipment had just been shut off. Yes,

Limestone Mill, Bloomington—Monroe Co. (423.13)

Limestone Mill (Circular saw.), Monroe Co. (101.08)

there was deterioration and vandalism, as well some jungle-like plant growth. Despite this, it seemed as if the workers had simply left for the day, and would be back in the morning. But, the doors were closed and the workers never would return to these forsaken places.

110   As I walked through each silent mill, under rusting beams and girders, over broken window glass, my shoes covered with limestone dust, I could almost hear the echoes of voices.

Limestone Mill (Hand wheels.), Monroe Co. (101.07)

111

Limestone Mill (Flywheels.), Bloomington—Monroe Co. (424.11)

Richmond Gas Company (Built in 1855 and placed on the National Register of Historic Places in 1981.), Richmond—Wayne Co. (715.09)

McCray Refrigeration (Founded in 1890, closed in 1998.), Kendallville—Noble Co. (775.02)

114

August Meyer Undertaker Shop (Built in 1912. Used by two generations of Meyers until the 1950s for embalming, showing caskets, and storing tents and other supplies.)—rural Dubois Co. (699.08)

Store, Pulaski—Pulaski Co. (782.10)

Store, New Corydon—Jay Co. (756.01)

115

116

Starr Piano Factory (Built in 1878, closed in 1949. Starr's record label, Gennett Records, issued recordings of jazz pioneers such as Louis Armstrong, Duke Ellington, Jelly Roll Morton, and Fats Waller.), Richmond—Wayne Co. (061.08)

Support structure for a Screening Plant (Used for grading and separating gravel at a gravel pit.), Martinsville—Morgan Co. (499.03)

AN OVERGROWN RUIN

At one time, the Terre Haute area had a number of brick and tile factories which, over the years, went through a series of mergers and closings. I couldn't learn much about the history of the one Lynn and I visited—The American Tile Co.—but I know it quit producing at least several decades ago. In fact, it was so overgrown we had difficulty walking around the site. A very large complex, with two tall chimneys, it was in sad condition. There was a central heating plant, which once blew hot air through shallow underground tunnels into each kiln, where the brick or clay tile was fired. Some tunnels had collapsed, so we had to watch each step we took.

The arch-shaped kilns had arch-shaped doors, and the kilns were all connected together in a long row. Some were in danger of collapsing.

After American Tile was shut down, the Michigan Mushroom Co. began raising mushrooms inside the kilns, which had the perfect climate for the purpose. That's why we found wooden doors on some of the kilns—they'd been added later and had been fine for growing fungi, but would have burned up if bricks were being fired. Eventually, the mushroom company also closed its doors—and the old factory has been at the mercy of the elements ever since.

The American Tile Co. (Interior of kiln.), West Terre Haute—Vigo Co. (640.07)

The American Tile Co., West Terre Haute—Vigo Co. (185.05)

The American Tile Co., West Terre Haute—
Vigo Co. (640.15)

The American Tile Co., West Terre Haute—
Vigo Co. (185.15)

Navarra Wholesale Grocery (Loading dock in alley.), Greensburg—Decatur Co. (711.08)

Schafer Glove Factory (Had been in business for nearly a century. Later a hardware supplier.),
Decatur—Adams Co. (755.01)

121

Stores, Petroleum—Wells Co. (768.08)

Stores, Birdseye—Dubois Co. (714.04)

Store, Boswell—Benton Co. (730.15)

Store, Jolietville—Hamilton Co. (700.06)

125

Grocery Store (Owned and operated, in succession, by Ad Hinds, Jeff Rayle, Burl Helton, Ralph Deckard, Vasel Eads, and Frank Stewart.), Handy—Monroe Co. (735.05)

A Century of Furniture

The Keller Manufacturing Co., in Corydon, was originally founded in 1885, by German immigrants, to produce spokes for the wheels of farm wagons. Later, they manufactured the entire wagon for International Harvester. Then, after the great Depression, Keller switched to furniture production. But Keller was versatile, and during WW II they even made walk-in ice boxes for the Army. Then, in mid-2003, after over a cen-

Keller Manufacturing Co. (Conveyor.), Corydon— Harrison Co. (726.06)

tury, Keller announced that it would be closing the Corydon plant. When Lynn and I visited in the summer of 2007, the buildings were almost empty. The saws, planers, sanders, etc. had been removed.

I did find a conveyor that wound its way through what appeared to be a finishing area. I was surprised it hadn't been sold off, as so much had been. As I explored further, taking pictures, I came to a room filled with all manner of electrical equipment. The largest pieces looked like giant motors. One was huge—almost as tall as I was.

A few days later, I telephoned Bob Hubbard, who retired from Keller after 40 years of service, to ask what all that electrical apparatus was for. Bob said I'd been in the Power Room, and what I'd seen were electric generators. There were also the remains of two steam engines, and various electrical controls.

Back in 1953, when Bob first started working at Keller, the company burned all its scrap wood and sawdust in a boiler, to create steam, which ran the two steam engines, which, in turn, ran the two electrical generators. The larger generator was an AC (alternating current) model, and it powered the saws and other machinery inside the factory. The smaller generator produced DC (direct current) for an outdoor sawmill. According to Bob, this power system eventually became outdated. The smaller DC generator was taken out of service first, followed by the AC unit in the 1980s. After that, Keller bought all its electricity.

By the time I photographed the old Power Room, some of the electrical controls, and giant knife switches had been removed, and other essential parts had been vandalized. The old generators and steam engines were badly deteriorated and useless. Today, they're all gone, and the Keller factory has been leveled.

126

Keller Manufacturing Co. (Power room.), Corydon—Harrison Co. (725.10)

Keller Manufacturing Co., Corydon—Harrison Co. (726.08)

127

128

Store, near Bath—Franklin Co. (771.15)

Wilkinson General Store (Was at various times a Hardware Store, a Grocery, and a Hat Shop.), Wallace—Fountain Co. (729.11)

129

Sluder's Auto Repair Shop/Standard Oil Station, Coalmont—Clay Co. (706.08)

General Store and Grocery, Green Oak—Fulton Co. (784.09)

132

General Store, Grange Corner—Parke Co. (730.02)

133

Store, Dunkirk—Jay Co. (769.01)

A Retired Spa

Martinsville—City of Mineral Water. So proclaims a neon sign, atop a building across from the Courthouse. Back in the late 1800s, this Morgan County town boasted a dozen spas (then known as sanatoriums) where out-of-towners drank and bathed in the local "healthy" water. Today, just two spa buildings remain, and John and I visited the one that was closed.

Martinsville Sanatorium, Martinsville—Morgan Co. (722.09)

First a little history. In 1898, an Indianapolis bicycle manufacturer named Bellis purchased two adjacent sanatoriums. By merging the Artesian Sanatorium into the Martinsville Sanatorium, he created one large, popular resort but, in 1913, it was badly damaged by a flood. Five years later, Bellis sold the water-ravaged spa to his son-in-law, Walter Kennedy.

Kennedy gave the place a new name—Martinsville Mineral Springs—and made some elaborate plans. By 1928, the spa was reborn as an impressive, block-long, brick structure, within a short stroll of the railroad station. Tudor Revival in style, it could accommodate as many as 150 guests. It was promoted as "One of the Three Best Known Watering Places in America"—and it probably was.

134

However, after the local spas lost their popularity, Kennedy donated his to the National Benevolent Association of the Disciples of Christ Churches in 1957. They converted the building into a retirement community called The Kennedy Memorial Home. When John and I were given permission to photograph the old resort, the retirement home had moved out (into a newer building next door), and only 20% of the 1928 building remained—its fate unknown.

As we wandered around, we found hardwood floors covered by worn carpet, and a mahogany staircase and woodwork coated with layers of paint. Yet, some details from the old days remained, such as a small, beautifully tiled niche that once served up mineral water.

I found the doors of the upper-level guest rooms of particular interest. Because the spa was constructed before air conditioning, each room had two lockable doors in the same frame—one was solid, the other louvered. When guests wanted cross ventilation, they would simply open their window, close the louvered door, then swing the solid door out of the way.

Martinsville Sanatorium, Martinsville—Morgan Co. (721.09)

On the main floor, just inside the arch-topped front windows, we discovered a hodgepodge of worn-out, hospital-style beds—a sad commentary on the decline of this once-proud place.

Martinsville Sanatorium (Second floor.),
Martinsville—Morgan Co. (722.06)

Martinsville Sanatorium (Water dispenser.),
Martinsville—Morgan Co. (721.08)

Martinsville Sanatorium (Hospital beds.), Martinsville—Morgan Co. (721.07)

Standard Oil Pumping Station (This 1888 facility was used to boost the pressure in a pipeline connecting Ohio with East Chicago. The large building contained steam engines, the small building was a telegraph station.), Lomax—Starke Co. (752.13)

137

Armours Creamery (Became Crystal Dairy in the 1960s.), Rochester—Fulton Co. (784.01)

138

Myers' Lanes Bowling Alley, Logansport—Cass Co. (794.13)

139

Judy's Carry-Out Restaurant, Shirley—Hancock Co. (780.09)

Ben Hur Building/Wolfe Hotel, New Amsterdam—Harrison Co. (563.05)

140

141

Mattingly's Canning Factory (Previously Shepherd Lathe Co., originally American Tobacco Co. Warehouse.),
Rising Sun—Ohio Co. (738.04)

142

Store, Templeton—Benton Co. (731.05)

When Lynn and I published our first book of Indiana photography in 2003—*Lingering Spirit*—or our second—*Guardians of the Soul*—in 2004, we didn't realize we were creating a series. But with this, our fifth book, it certainly seems to be turning out that way.

Nor did we imagine we'd cover so many miles—or visit so many interesting places. In the process of completing our third book, *2nd Stories*, we passed through every Indiana town south of U.S. 40—the Old National Road. With book number four, *After the Harvest*, we drove through scores of towns in the northern half of the state as well. So, by the time we were ready to start on *Silent Workplace*, we decided that, when we were in particular area, following up on a lead, we'd just check out any nearby towns we'd never been to before.

As a result, since starting work on *Lingering Spirit*, we've driven over 65,000 miles, and we've visited every single city and town in Indiana. To document this feat, we've marked up an official 2004 Indiana State Highway Map, and crossed off every single town shown—all 2,099 of them. There were metropolises, medium-sized cities, small burgs, and places where all that was left was a pair of stop signs. In a couple of instances, there weren't even any stop signs. In our humble opinion, if there's nothing left, the town should be expunged—particularly when there are other communities, consisting of a store and a few houses, that aren't on the State highway map.

Actually, more-detailed county maps show a number of such hamlets—and we've been to more than a few of them. But we're going to stick with the 2,099 figure as our official number.

Some of the towns we visited had the same name. For example, there are three Mechanicsburgs, two Scipios, a pair of Bunker Hills, and two towns called Five Points. There are over a dozen communities known by two different names. One of the four Mt. Pleasants also goes by the name of Hazel, Laud also goes by Forest, and Borden and New Providence are the same place. There are four Salems (one of which also goes by Steele) and there's a Salem Center. Of the colors, Green is particularly popular—there are 15 cities and towns containing a Green, ranging from Greenbriar, to Greenfield Mills, to Greens Fork to Greenwood. There are only five places with Brown in their name, but seven containing White. And each one of the 2,099 is unique.

Now that we've covered the entire state, we've been asked if that's enough, are we finished exploring Indiana. To which we reply "not hardly!" You see, as we've driven around, we've generally been looking for specific subjects, for a particular book. So, we've driven right by some excellent photo-ops—and not stopped. If we'd have photographed everything of interest, we'd never have had enough time to complete the current project. So, Lynn has been making notes about places we'd like to return to some day, and there are many unexplored back roads that still beckon. In short, we've got a lot more discovering to do—and more photographs to take.

AFTERWORD

Whenever we meet someone new, one of the first things we learn about them is what they do for a living. "Hi, I'm so-and-so, and I'm a teacher (or machinist, or waitress, or lawyer, or nanny)." We do this because what-we-do is considered a summary of who-we-are.

If an individual says they're a doctor, we conjure up an immediate image, one that's different from that of a hair stylist, foundry worker, or accountant. In short, knowing what a person does for a living, gives us a sampling of their personality, perhaps their level of education, maybe even an idea of where, and how, they live.

Sometimes, I catch myself guessing the occupations of others. For example, if I'm waiting in line, I'll speculate about the people around me. There's a man in jeans and T-shirt, with a dark tan—he probably does outdoor manual labor. Or that woman wearing an expensive blue suit—she could be an executive.

In a related manner, when I wander around a closed-up business, I find myself visualizing the men and women who worked there. It's not their faces I see, but what they wore, and what they did, week after week—sometimes for decades. By standing where they stood, where they spent their days (or nights on a graveyard shift), I feel I can get a picture of who they were.

Of course, I know I'm relying on preconceived ideas, guesswork, and stereotypes, as we all do.

No occupation can completely define anyone—not what a person reads, the music he listens to, or what food she prefers. It reveals nothing about a spouse, children, pets, or hobbies. Despite this, we continue to identify others, and ourselves, by how a paycheck is earned—it's *almost* who we are.

Because the silent workplaces on these pages have been central to the identities of so many owners and employees, over so many years, I feel these empty buildings are physical monuments to those lives. They are visible, tangible examples of our state's working legacy, and are essential to our collective Hoosier identity. They're not just derelict structures from an earlier time, but the material remains of once-vital enterprise, and they need to be honored.

As a final note, I'd like to warmly thank Gayle and Bill Cook for sharing their perceptive observations and commentary in the Foreword to *Silent Workplace*. The Cooks have restored a wide range of Indiana's fading commercial buildings. And they deeply appreciate their importance to those who came before us, those living today, and to all who will come after. I'm grateful to have them as a part of this book.   —JB

Bear Brand Hosiery Co., Gary—Lake Co. (752.02)

144